PETER JAY

THE LAST BRIGHT APPLE

Peter Jay

The Last Bright Apple

POEMS 1962–2024

Grey Suit Editions

First published in 2025
by Grey Suit Editions, an affiliate
of Karnac Books Ltd

British Library Cataloguing in Publication Data
A C.I.P. catalogue record for this book is available
from the British Library

Paperback ISBN: 978-1-903006-41-2
e-book ISBN: 978-1-903006-42-9

Designed and set in Monotype Ehrhardt by Anvil

Printed and bound in the United Kingdom
by Hobbs the Printers Ltd

Grey Suit Editions
33 Holcombe Road, London N17 9AS
https://greysuiteditions.co.uk/

T.

Like the sweet apple that reddens on the topmost branch,
at the tip of the topmost branch, missed by the pickers;
no, not missed by them, but they could not reach it –

SAPPHO

Contents

Shifting Frontiers (1980)

1 *Beginnings*

2 *Lifelines*

Intermezzo

Changes (1971–2024)

Shifting Frontiers

I

Beginnings

First Love

If the spring had not come
and melted my breath

I would have known what lay beyond
the hills when we wandered them

and knew only the silence,
the terror of dawn, lifting

my utmost prayer to the light,
as the spring raised

my breathing over the hills
into the pure and fire

The Mirror

So that I might
precisely retain
that moment, perfectly
fulfilling itself,
now
only a vague
form in fugitive
moods, a
memory, blurred –

Morning, I
travel-worn,
you idly resting,
two garden chairs
drawn up,
and the detail
is lost; only
images
later recurring:

The sun's liquid rim
a pool
of melted gold
caught in a glass,
like a word
said and unsaid

too quickly –
echoing
ever more faintly for ever.

Palinurus

We left the sleeping harbour draped in flames.
The moral of this furnace is to prove
The only catalyst for love is love.
The games we play are always funeral games.

Shorten the sail, set the canvas aslant
To the wrenching wind. There's safety in our oars,
Though further funerals wait at all the shores
We reach to capture with the lives we spend.

A drowsy hand now beckons me to sleep,
Relax my limbs into the fold of deep
Enclosing waves. What's an old helmsman for
When those young warriors reach the Italian shore?
Drop to the sea, back to your mother's breast
And in the lap of waves you'll be at rest.

The Alchemist

Analysis exploding lies untold,
The broken filter drips. In acid pain
Imagination had turned you to gold.

The process was to carry out controlled
Experiments; then art could later feign
Analysis, exploding lies untold.

A silver moon once gave your head the cold
Beauty of marble; when I looked again
Imagination had turned you to gold.

Try as I might to strain and save the old
Solutions, they grew weak, could not contain
Analysis exploding, lies untold.

Too late to sift what's faint, that once was bold:
The still-born ashes of a mind's mundane
Imagination had turned you to gold.

Lover or phoenix, all can turn a mould
To new translation, by dissolving vain
Analysis, exploding lies; untold
Imagination had turned you to gold.

Variation on a Theme from Pushkin

I loved you. Would you hate me if you knew?
To tell you so, I never could have dared
For once, you know, I wanted to be you.

Your awkward grace I'd grown accustomed to,
Yet was afraid to ask you if you cared;
Perhaps your reticence meant that you knew

I loved you. Was there nothing you could do
But smile to prove what innocence we shared?
For once, you know, I wanted to be you.

Remembering

When cool shadows close the day
Sweeping busy noise away,
And rewarding sleep brings peace
To suburban terraces,
Restless as the hours drag on
I lie, waiting for the dawn.
In the quiet dread of dark
Anguish pricks me like a snake
Biting deep into my heart;
Pulses drumming, bitter thought
Swamps my mind, and memory's
Tape plays back before my eyes.
Trembling as I hear the story
I complain with wounded fury,
Poisoned curses, till I sweat
Shedding tears of vain regret –
Tears that can't wipe out the sorrow
When the tape unwinds tomorrow.

after Pushkin

Envy

I'm jealous. So far
        it's a secret
                I haven't told anyone.
I know there's a boy
        living somewhere
                I'm really envious of.
I envy his manner –
        you'd never find me
                so open, so naturally
sincere.
        I envy him too the way
                he laughs –
when I was young
        I could never
                laugh like that.
He's always covered
        with bumps and scratches –
                I
was neater and tidier,
        thoroughly
                spotless.
And all the places in books
        that I used to skip
                he ploughs through.

I have to admit he's better
in this way too: he's
uncompromisingly honest –
won't tolerate evil
out of good nature.
When I slam down my pen
saying, 'No
it's not worth it...'
he'll pick up his and say
'Let's have a go.'
And if there's a knot
he can't untie
he cuts it.
I never bother
with either.
When he falls in love
it sticks. I
fall in and out.
I shall conceal my envy –
smile –
pretend to be
naïve: 'Who is there
to smile to?
For whom should I change
my *modus vivendi*?'
– But however I try
to convince myself

('We all have
our own lives to lead . . .')
I shall never
forget that somewhere
there's a boy who'll achieve
more than I shall.

after Yevtushenko

Fear

I

In the still void preceding the immense
Outburst of pain, when like a dynamo
The silence hums, I heard a small voice grow
Inside me, focusing to an intense
Pitch, battering against the lungs' taut wall.
I feared the knowledge, not the actual fall.
And losing heart was far the worst of all.

For two weeks I remained in hospital.
The pain receded. I would watch the birds
Daily fly in and tour the busy wards,
Picking at crumbs. They brought a personal
Remorse with them, those kindly visitors.
They came within like stern inquisitors
Accusing me, where fear was general.

The old wound bleeds again. Some others came,
Friends as I called them, bringing grapes or beer;
And I could barely make them feel at home,
Yet could not hide, nor let them know my fear.
'Tomorrow you'll feel better; read the book
I gave you yesterday – it's worth a look.'
(Inside me, something almost lifeless shook.)

Daily they came, the friendly ones I love,
Exacting retribution in a verse
Paid to the unknown god. And still his swallow
Beats home my failure, circling as I nurse
My silent heart god-wounded, since Apollo
Deserted me and left those birds above
To harass springtime with a lovely curse.

Is this the expression of a common pain
Renewed, or a new struggle to explain
What was not felt before? Rhetorical
The question may be, yet the answer's real.
However near the thing may come, I feel
Its presence most in distance mocking me:
Who feared the mountains, never saw the sea.

As for the sea, I saw; but did not hear
Its straight applause; what I heard was a scream
Less plausible, seeming to hit my ear
With spitfire consonants that bit my shame:
'This great Homeric sound you will not match;
Stay in the gentle plains, where you may catch
The trickling vowels of some smaller stream.'

2

In soft September, when the year revives
New melancholies, and late apples fall
Like blossom, autumn's surfeit for brocade,

I walked back from the woods into a hall
Where childhood's myth in adult fiction lives.
What I saw was a world gone weary, all
The ripeness one man wore had now decayed.

O children, children, will you forget the day
When death walked in his halting steps, whose pace
The quick years and the unexpected stroke
Slackened too soon, until one day he broke
Down, and we saw him crippled? Pray, pray
That he may walk now in the halls of grace,
And from his grave abode bid us peace.

But if the tumbling months should yet allow
Some later crop of roses to persist
When all the clay has crumbled, we should grow
Adequate in acceptance, and resist
Joining the disillusioned who but see
The sorrow underlying gaiety.
Uncastled from detachment, let us not follow

The slow procession wearing its mask awry,
Which, silent, throngs the dismal plain, and fears
The mortal skeleton behind frail skin
Opening to the march of quicker years
Through angry Aprils into guilty May;
Afraid to let the angelic stranger in,
Or hear the whispering voice; or, heard, obey.

3

Shadows of things still haunt us: forms of love
Now broken, cracked, divided; yet a laugh
May prove a diamond mirrored in a pool,
Mind's eye may obliquely capture – though the light
Behind grows fainter, and ahead the future
Flows on with stronger tide; so may some hint
Flash, as we turn, and dazzle with its glint.

Whiter than snow, the crystal thoughts return.
It is the stranger brings these later flowers.
Await his coming, for you stand alone...
The pride of youth locked you in its prison.
You wait on alien, cruel or kindly, powers;
Appease them, let love serve; a higher reason
Serves your obedience to the godlike towers.

Closer. Stay with me, yet a little while;
For some can love and never let it show
And leave before the time they have to go,
Stretching a human inch into a mile
Of dull indifference. And then, alert,
The furious angels stand by, to assert
Their presence only in your absent smile.

Exorcize silence: I have had enough.
Let us come to reasonable terms. Now I give
That you may give – these catalogues of grief

I hand you, praying: expiate now my rough
Seas with a calming breath; let order thrive;
Let the strange angel bring the unseen leaf,
And in return I shall obey with love.

And when night lifts the curtain to reveal
Beings outside my world, men in disguise
Who play the parts we only know are real
Because the light is relative to dark,
I shall close back the blinds, and turn my eyes
To shelter where my birds, friends, shadows flock
Into an unbarred, flowered paradise.

And let the hysterical assault on my eardrums
Cease; and all the nightlong screaming of children
Be soothed, soothed; gentle nurse, find them peace;
When they cry blindly they are choking dreams,
The waking pain is nightmare; terror seems
To paralyse their flocks; now let the sheep
Float over fences, drifting them to sleep.

Newdigate Prize, Oxford University, 1965

Absence

What is a poet?
All that remains of his poem.

September already. Evenings mild
with disappointment; the breeze
passes, leaves
a whisper suspended

It is to copy the meaning of slight words returned

amid the press of words,
the unconsidered, the hurtful,
convenient devaluations for comfort,
grand promises to toast, daily
bread but no word

and are all the temples for sale?

Or the ripe wind, the pledge?
the love-link suspended,
the Word untouched by words

Sunlight, *la mer d'Italie*,
the broken walls of a city
lava-sunk – my eyes were rolling all night

but I saw nothing,
swimming in your dark eyes, blinded with light.

And meeting again, it will be
all that is left of this poem
greeting you, simply.

Morning

At morning, when the mist
rises, and dew is crystal on each
stiff grass-blade, and the coral
air is unchilled by the sun's
tentative rays, raising
my eyes from the river, where
on the mirrored disc I had let
moments flicker, for with this quickening
day it is spring –

Exhausted, I drink in
life from the waking day, reflect
at ease on the long night breaking into love.

Brief Seasons

for Brs Simon and Jerome

1

Green, green, it is still
Green – a leaf, so
Many new leaves to turn!

2

Warm seas and wine
And our idle happiness:
Will we ever be in love?

3

The sun drops deep, a breeze
Breaks the contour of cedars –
No beating of swallow wings.

4

Skeleton trees, winds rave,
Paths shine like distant rivers
Immersed in contemplation.

The Notable Things

My fashion's been to note the notable things
In their own shape, where shape might lend some kind
Impression, an eloquent mode in which to find
Cause for the silence fond observance brings,
Or hesitant, breaks.
                                        How have I been wrong –
Listening to the sirens, not their song?

2

Lifelines

October Letter

How distant you seem to me now,
echo of an age more transitory
than childhood, than death! –

an enduring moment that passed
casually. And you went away,
hurt with the gradual fall of years;

grandiose and ridiculous
my dreams, their emendations
unadopted in the margin of laughter.

It is a tone
we struck: you
whom I never knew,

who never knew me, but by
that chord
infinitely sounded between us.

So now I acknowledge also
many occasions that never were,
words unspoken, incomplete

gestures, the timeless
nature of unknown intimacy
wasted. How close we are now!

(The echoing spell binds me
absolutely: a secret, too,
quite without sound.)

Homage to Mimnermos

for Peter Whigham

On matters of love Mimnermos is worth more than Homer,
Love is a civilized god looking for gentle songs.

— SEXTUS PROPERTIUS

I

Life, what is life, what is pleasure
            without Aphrodite the golden?
O let me die when my heart
Cares no more for these things –
Soft beds and the secret gifts of lovers,
Youth's brief flower
            a joy to all men and women.

Age advances, chanting a dirge,
            befouling man and his heart,
He is torn within and without,
Anxiety strips the sun from his eyes,
            disfigures his mind,
Evil is sown within him.
His children hate him, women lose their respect,
Death takes him by disease
            or cuts him off childless
Wanting children more than life.

2

As the sun unfolds dawn
        rising from his gold chamber
Youth ripens overnight.

Then we were innocent leaves under sunbeams,
With knowledge neither of good nor evil.

But when ripeness ebbs in slow decrepitude
It is better to die than remain living.

3

And youth like a dream, the sun in the sky
Climbing with labour,
Nor does he rest from his labour
Until in the evening he floats back to dawn
        on a slow wave of sleep,
And all we are asking is death at a pleasant age
Painless, swift as a dream.

Youth, precious youth, stay with the sun
Climbing the sky; at day's end
There is no end of rising pain in the heart.

Youth like a dream, sweat on my flesh,
I tremble to see the blossom of my generation,

Even the sun
Bows down to rest on the Ocean's lips,
And his horses are gone till daybreak.

Once

Fragments, the long avenue,
            noise of radios, bells,
a rain-soaked garden
            late May perhaps,
I could invest the scene
            with evidence
gathered then
            now circumstantial
imagined even, but what
            I remember is
we met: drowsy with memories
            forgotten now, if
ever substantial; half
            in love, having never
touched each other, we drank
            by the river in sunlight, crossed
the bridge and talked until
            we could no longer
divert leave-taking.
            Half in love what is love
I remember I love you still
            though have forgotten
all but the moment
            which detained me
which we abandoned.

Indecision

All the time he was waiting
for an attack of inspiration,
observing things with a languid
yet perceptibly poetic distraction,
the said things seem to have been
watching him with the curious
eyes of a cat who wonders
if you will possibly stroke him.

Adrift

Suspended as between dreaming and sleep
Or between waking and dream, sleep and waking
Our bodies neither waking nor dreaming nor sleeping
Separate, and we linger in love’s wake.

Ezra Pound 1970

These last drafts
          no lees but finest vintage,
fragments, splinters
          of the unattainable
crystal, in their refraction
          more than a little light,
          a little rightness.

Clarity, simplicity
          against the murk –

And as from a dynamo running down
          to silence, the final sparks
spin off – a flickering eloquence
          flares out through the darkness

Heroes, luminous air and the current
          flowing through for an instant,
the spell of the temple and all live things
          singing eternal,
the deeps in you, cohering.

Solitary

I see the glint in your eyes,
The ring on your finger.

Solo

Midnight,
        the small hours
wandering on

        and the thin
memories waken
        still warm

thickening as
        the small rain
swells – alone

        the slow night
dwindles as you turn
        in, lingering, till

idly at last
        you lie, drained
of longing.

Losing Touch

These things that grow unclear: the slow-burning
After-image of you unfocusing,
Like a figure blurring rapidly in a mist –
And once more you are lost, and drift away
Light-years each second into the negative dark,
And I am left
Blinded with that bright snapshot, a shadow torn
Out of my mind.

Eros to Psyche

Sometimes the image of her comes at night
Walking toward him in a film of light
Alone, in his own darkness, till he wakes
And the flimsy semblance breaks –
He shelters once more under sleep's dipped wing,
But she shines on in his imagining.

To Psyche

Unguarded soul, you hover
lightly above her head
who knew no lack of lover
till one came with wings spread.

Soul, when their flesh conspires
by candle-light, don't cry
for her: the love-flame lures
you too, and you must fly.

Six Poems after Faiz

for Alison

Last Night

A blown rose out of season,
The stealthy advent of spring in a desert,
The faint shuffling of a breeze over sand –
Last night
The memory of you came from afar and stroked me,
Like peace calling on a sick man, without reason.

When She Comes to Mind

In the caress of this morning breeze
Her fingers touch me. Then as it lifts, I feel
Her hands move outward, gathering those we love,
Searching for the hidden wound in their hearts.

Since the Long Days

Since the long days of long-lost expectation
Your image resides in that alien spring
Where far from your embrace, your eyes, your arms
I am still held with unfamiliar longing.

Loneliness

Tonight my close companion, loneliness
Attends me and pours out my glass of wine.
We sit outside, watch for the moon to rise
And raise your image rustling in the shadows.

Lullaby

Midnight, moon and oblivion,
Earth but a play of dead shadows,
A torrent of silence echoing
The moonlight's exhausted murmur –
And still my desire is not stilled.
O lonely fellowship of stars!

O faint lamentation! The leaves
Continue their monologue, cold
Legends of selfless devotion.
And you, my heart's mirage? And you?

Idyll

Road, arcade of trees, houses, the roof's rim.
Up there the moon quietly bares her breast
As if shedding a gown unbuckled.
A stagnant blue lake of shadows, a leaf
Drifting across, a pricked bubble that vanishes.
A hand was pouring wine into my glass –
Rose-water, rose of your hands, fingers like petals
Stroking me for a moment,
My heart repeating soft familiar words,
And 'Softly!' you whispered,
'Softer!' the moon breathed, leaning down.

To W.H. Auden, October 1973

Though summoned unpunctually to a state beyond words
Know, if the soul translated from its familiar
Mask can care as it did for our mundane cares,
That we inherit a hoard which time cannot tax, since
Aphony was not your habit. If seemly the stillness
Now in our hearts, you will interrupt it; not life and
    words but
Death and silence are temporary.

In Memory of Pastoral

tibi Palinure

Closing time in the gardens of the west:
Dusk thoughts among old trees
In the vineyards of the soul. Where shall we go
When all the doors of Europe shut behind us?
Brightness has fallen from the air,
Only the sibilant wind through pines
And the static of cicadas at midday
Gather among the ruins. Here
Daphnis died, and Aphrodite ran
Mourning forever in Meropian Cos,
Where now the white marks of a dark spring day
Disfigure the hillside, et in Arcadia
Spirit and stones lie broken.

The Gallery

for Harry Guest

Slowly they assemble, one
by one: some whose faces
shine with the smile of certain
gestures long-recalled,
others in the shadowed recesses
insubstantial; rare,
rarest of loves, who never
left their visible imprint,
but who appear for a moment
fitfully incarnate –
never to be acknowledged, or
tamed in the heart. In the still
centre, the mind's gallery,
I salute all who are absent.

Little Langdale

to Richard Holmes

Swans on the tarn
move with the weather,
rain, wind or sun,
drifting together.

Evening: cross over
the mountain ridge,
down by the river
to the slate bridge,

up to the stone
cottage. We play
cards, and fortune
smiles on us equally.

I would like words to be
clean as this life,
free as the water,
strong as the earth.

The Years

Intimate memoranda, your touch
lingering with me, glimpse
of a sunlit lawn long ago,
vestigial presences. How do lives
ever connect? But gently, beyond
years, distances. Nothing between us,
only the clasp of your hand
undermining my silence.

A Game of Chess

in memory of C.H.O'D. Alexander

Plot and counterplot, maze
of possible lines, threads
to unravel, silent
conspiracies: my brain
reels, there is no certain
path. Abortive attack,
likely defences, ebb
and flow – if this, but that
then this; combinations
surfacing in the web
of thought, half-seen. Beyond
the calculable, one
prays for deliverance
from evil. Wait; then push
the pawn forward, hoping.

Matins

An unopened packet of French Toast,
A breakfast coffee cup
Its hairline crack betraying
Years of use, so neatly stacked away –
All the ingredients of my daily bread
Possess me with their absences.
Until this loss of faith is ended
There's nothing more to do.
The observances are suspended.

Lifelines

to Joseph Brodsky, for our joint birthday

Fragments about the lost or dead
Hung in the air; wandering overhead
A disembodied voice drawled on
Snaring our talk with talk of revolution.
You groped for foreign words, orphaned
In a cold bar, a solitary no-man's-land,
    And haltingly you read to me
    Translating your translation of *The Flea*.
    What's freedom but the rule of poetry?

Such separate worlds in this combine,
Making a new world, neither yours nor mine,
Where sense may apprehend and search
What we in our twin closed spheres cannot reach.
So we are entangled, when we've done
Marvelling at the quick net of a pun,
    In the still life of poetry,
    Through which we climb to common territory
    By lifelines rhymed in triple sympathy.

Life of the Pawn

to Ştefan Aug. Doinaş

'les Pions . . . sont l'âme des Echecs' – PHILIDOR

Forward at first – two steps.
Then more cautiously, one
pace only when protected. Now
the time comes to resist, facing
attack from every angle.
We may too recklessly take up
a forward, exposed position,
or under restraint behave
too timidly. Nevertheless
we have strength in numbers,
we have to be closely watched.
The majority of us accept
passive rôles; motionless
we may appear to be, but
we give each other support.
Though we can never retreat
we know how to stand still.
We capture deviously.
                                        Sometimes
we are sacrificed in a cause,
not knowing precisely why;
for us, in general, the game's
the thing, since we know the outcome
is usually decided by other

stronger forces. More often though
we are lost in desperation
or simply abandoned, picked off.

But we have aspirations. Clear
our paths and on we press –
step by step creating
delicate shifts in the balance
of power. Not threatening
in ourselves, we can seem
to threaten to become threats
that cannot be dealt with.

In the end just one of us can
be enough to decide everything.

Murals

ut pictura poesis

I

White space on the dark side of the world
What lives within your walls? You are blank,
Uncharted. The air is always cloudless above you,
The mountains surround you, they are icily blue.
When sleep dissolves your mistress's sight
And she escapes from herself, do you hold her captive,
Open your ivory gates, let the moonlight in
Admitting her dreams, your only inhabitants?

2

From my window beyond the mountains I see her
In the green world, branches shredding sunlight
Over her bed, her body mingling with body
And we invade each other, I become her
Whispering an echo of leaves which tangle.

3

When she goes I am nothing. She won't see me
Pale, immured in a surface, overlooking
The rumpled trees, her bed I would enter nightly
Waiting for her who grants me a soul. She comes,
The sunlight enters me before I dwindle,
Brief the breath from her lips that revives me, gone now.

Provisional Poem

I think of the gentlest people I have known,
you are among them. In my colourless dreams
I am a butterfly, you are a stone
picked from a river-bank after centuries,
imaginably beautiful and unique.
I have no memory of my memories,
bare white rooms furnished with antique loves
untenanted and irrecoverable.
The universe exists in a stone,
there are stones in the memory of things,
stones remember their butterfly existence
and I exist in the memory of stones.
Talking and silence do not change these things
nor the necessity of daily life.
To love things, to know them as they are,
never to know the colour of your eyes.

Wingless Eros

for Judy

She gave me wings to fly

Wings like hers of a hummingbird
hovering by the red flowers
invisible wings on which
to fly to the green land of Nod

She anointed my shoulders with unguents
delicate juices to nurture
the slender fabric of promise

Three nights I slept
and three nights dreamed of flight
but when I woke on the fourth day
my wings could not be believed

In Transit

To anticipate the past, to start
Again from your destination,
That would be better. But best
Would be again to be back
At your point of departure,
Remembering the future.

Vigils

for Judy

Four thousand miles from home,
From the shifting frontiers of thirty years,
From the habitual lives we do not like
But love, my friend lies close
In the no-man's-land of sleep.
I wonder, as she stirs
What ghosts burst through her guard,
Posturing wildly with white flags or guns –
Would like to assume powers
To stop and search, but let them pass
As a smile turns the corner of her mouth.

Ars Politica

for Paul and Hualing Nieh Engle

What can be done with poets?
Such awkward people. We know
They don't matter at all; why then
Do they concern us? They write,
They think, they talk to each other.
A few people read them. And that
Makes them dangerous?
Put them in jail, give them prizes!

Bad Weather

(TUNE: BACOVIAN)

for Nichita

Persistent rain. The heart
settles for second-best,
for emptiness, for dormancy,
for limp, resistant rest.

Vocatives remain unheard.
It is hard to keep awake.
The mind inhabits heavy limbs,
the damp systems creak.

Mist sinks in around the edges,
the rain talks in stutters,
I sit alone, and drearily
pick idle rhymes, write letters.

Distant friends feel closer, yet
the landscape will not change.
Lead, the cryptic river, foregone
optative, sleep. Your name.

Déja Vu

a painting in the Art Institute, Chicago

You were there to the life.
I thought of all those dreary Greek poems
about how you could almost believe
someone's portrait would talk to you
if you spoke to it. Even the truth
will not bear so much repetition.
You were there framed in a bed,
answering none of my questions,
and I turned from you again
just as angry and speechless,
wanting the cool street air.

Beliefs

Believe it was all a lie.
Believe that I never really
understood you at all.
Believe that you are not wanted.
Believe that you were deceived.
Believe that my life with you was
a pretence, if you like, believe
that I simply took you for granted.
Believe what you want to believe.
Believe that we still have a chance.
Believe that I do not believe
myself. Believe if you can
that once we believed in a life
requiring no such beliefs.

Thinking of Friends with Whom I Do Not Keep in Touch

1 *'A romantic poet lost in a century of violence'*

Yes, Gerardo, I promise you *fog in London*
when you visit. Having no common language
we will converse in *famous poetry . . .*
We will *fly to heaven, that is the truth*, I believe it.

2 *Jorge*

If I do not reply to your incomprehensible postcards
it is because as you say *Everything is French!*
and I should like to offer you something to equal
Flesh, heaven, angels, poetry, and bestsellers!

Reading Brecht's Poems Soon after My Daughter's Birth

The passion, yes, and the care.
An end and a beginning.
For what is human let us be
Truly thankful.

Intermezzo

Nights on my bed…

Nights on my bed I searched for the man
        my soul loves – I
searched, but did not find him.
'I will get up and go round the town
        through the streets and squares
and hunt out the man I love.'

I looked, but could not find him.

Soldiers making their rounds in the town met me
('Have you seen the man I love?')
and I'd scarcely passed them when
        I finally found him.
I held him, I would not let go
till I had brought him back
        to mother's house
to the room of the woman who bore me.

By the gazelles and deer of the field
I make you swear, daughters of Jerusalem,
not to disturb or interrupt our love
till it is satisfied.

ANONYMOUS
from *The Song of Songs*

Par with the gods…

Par with the gods he seems, the man there
sitting with you face to face, closely
picking up your sweet
talk and enticing

laughter: that set my heart
fluttering. When for a moment
I look up and see you,
I can no longer

talk, my tongue sticks, under
my skin a sliver of flame
slips, eyes see nothing, ears
hum, and a chilling

sweat spreads across me, shivering
takes me over, paler now
than grass, I seem to be hardly
short of death –

but I must risk everything, since a poor
[ ]

SAPPHO

Bandusia

Spring more brilliant than crystal, claiming
homage of wine and flowers, tomorrow
you shall be given a kid, whose
forehead bulging with first

horns prefigures passion and battles
– in vain; for this sprig of a frisky herd
will taint your chill streams with the dark
dye of its crimson blood.

Untouched by the flaring dog-star's heatwaves
you are there, tendering plough-worn oxen
and lazily wandering flocks
your darling refreshment.

Through me you too will be a famous spring,
known for the oak that rests on the hollow
rocks, from which your fluent waters
laughingly patter down.

HORACE

Diffugere nives...

The snows are routed; now the grass returns
to fields, leaves to the trees;
Earth's order turns successively, and rivers
decrescendo to streams.
The Grace with twins and Nymphs now ventures out
naked to lead her choir.
Do not expect eternal orders, the year
warns, and the dayrobbing hour.
Frost coaxed to thaw; spring trampled underfoot
by summer – which is interred
When appled autumn spills its fruit; until
winter returns, inert.
Swift moons succeed, repair the failing skies.
We fall – and when we follow
Father Aeneas, Tullus the Rich and Ancus,
resemble dust and shadow.
Who knows if the gods will add tomorrow's time
to what this day is ours?
All things you grant your own dear soul escape
the grasping hands of heirs.
Once you are dead and Minos has decreed
his everlasting orders,
Neither your breeding, eloquence nor grace
can bring you back, Torquatus.

Diana will not let Hippolytus
    the prude escape her darkness,
No, nor can Theseus smash the chains of Lethe
    to save his loved Perithous.

HORACE

Animula vagula blandula

Vagabond delicate soul,
body's guest and companion,
what place must you enter now
numbed, colourless and naked –
not, in your old way, joking?

HADRIAN

Time

All that mother nature nursed into being,
however stable it seems, all gives way
whittled by time and continuous usage,
    brittle and frayed.

Rivers begin to run in strange valleys,
established paths no longer tenable
when banks burst in submission to the flood's
    tenacious piling.

Water hollows rough limestone by dripping,
the ploughshare's iron is thinned in the field,
golden finger-adorning rings are worn
    bright with attrition.

SULPICIUS LUPERCUS SERVASIUS IUNIOR

From Exile

When do you end, spring flower,
autumn moon? How much
of the past comes to mind. Last night
the east wind blew again
round the cottage. I cannot bear
turning back to my old country
when the moon is bright.

The carved railings, the marble
staircase are still there,
only those beautiful faces
have altered. And you ask
how much sadness one can take: just
as much as a river of spring
waters running east.

LI YU

Ballade of Women from the Past

Tell me where, in what realm is
that lovely Flora now, the Roman,
Archipiada, or Thaïs
her cousin and her very twin,
or Echo, speaking out just when
sound across pond or river flowed,
whose beauty was far more than human.
But where are the snows of old?

Where is that wise one, Eloïse,
for whom Pierre Abelard began
life as a monk at St Denis
after castration? This his pain
for love. And where too is the queen
who ordered Buridan to be hurled
in a sack into the river Seine?
But where are the snows of old?

And Queen Blanche, white as fleur-de-lis,
the singer with a siren's tone,
Bertha Big-foot, Beatrice, Alice,
Arembourg, heiress to Maine,
and the good Joan of Lorraine
burned by the English at Rouen,
where are they, Virgin sovereign?
But where are the snows of old?

Prince, don't ask me where they've gone
this week or this year, not for the world;
all you will get is this refrain:
But where are the snows of old?

FRANÇOIS VILLON

I Loved You

I loved you; with a love, perhaps, that's yet
Not altogether dampened in my soul;
But do not give it further troubled thought:
I do not want to sadden you at all.
I loved you silently and hopelessly,
Torn now by jealousy, now by reserve;
I loved you once so truly, tenderly
As may God grant you find another love.

ALEXANDER PUSHKIN

Fantasy

There is an air for which I'd give away
All of Rossini, Mozart, all Weber,
A very old, a yearning, funeral air,
One which has secret charms only for me.

And every time I chance to hear that tune,
Two hundred years are taken off my heart...
The time is Louis Treize; I see rolled out
A green hill, yellowed by the setting sun,

A rose-brick château cased in mellow stone,
Its panes of glass soft-stained with reddish hues,
Encircled by great gardens, with a stream
Lapping its feet, as it flows out through flowers;

Then at her lofty window she appears,
Blonde with black eyes, dressed in a bygone style,
The lady whom in another life perhaps
I have already seen... and recognize!

GÉRARD DE NERVAL

Lead

The coffins of lead were lying sound asleep,
And the lead flowers and the funeral clothes –
I stood alone in the vault... and there was wind...
And the wreaths of lead creaked.

Upturned my lead belovèd lay asleep
On the lead flowers... and I began to call –
I stood alone by the corpse... and it was cold...
And the wings of lead drooped.

Winter Dusk

Sombre and metallic, dusk in winter,
The whiteness of the plain – vast and round –
A raven comes rowing from the background,
Cutting the skyline at the diameter.

Occasional trees like crystal in their snow.
Longings for disappearance sip at me,
While the same raven goes back silently,
Cutting the skyline at the diameter.

GEORGE BACOVIA

Music

The music was bringing me close to things.
She set an arch between me and them
and I could fall from far, from spheres
without breaking a limb,
wasting not one drop of power.

Like a magnet the music picked from me
the coppery feeling, the feeling of violet.
It lifted them up, like blades
of sprouting grass.

And watching, he could see
a coppery field, a field of violet
above which slowly unfolds
the nocturnal chain of pale-blue stars,
under which,
temple to temple
rib to rib,
our lives embraced.

NICHITA STĂNESCU

Master Me

Master me completely, night!
Into your loose and darkly float-
ing waves, I wade out.
Within you wonderingly they roll
the burdens of their pallid souls,
the silent destitute.

However you may change above
the fraying world, still you are one,
eternal gentle solace;
all that's outside you falls apart,
and what your soft strength forces out
disintegrates to ash.

But you live; your star-images,
those ancient speechless figures, blaze
everywhere your power:
from you I came, just like the first
angels, and I in you exist;
grasp and absorb me now!

Forget all my unfaithfulness.
Unmasterable compulsions press
me back to you again;

you be the stream and I your foam,
admit your prodigal son home,
sombre, dark heaven.

Pathogeny and Swansong

A white arm from the snow-white mirror,
a fine, slight arm with unremitting power,
with a cold sponge from the cold glass
tries from time immemorial to make someone,
someone or something vanish.

JÁNOS PILINSZKY

Everything Changes

Everything changes. You can make
A fresh start with your final breath.
But what is done is done. And the water
That you poured into the wine, you cannot
Pour out again.

What is done is done. The water
That you poured into the wine, you cannot
Pour out again, but
Everything changes. You can make
A fresh start with your final breath.

BERTOLT BRECHT

Changes

(1980–2024)

There is only a single great life
in which we take part.
There is only a single great life –
for the rest, we are nothing.

NICHITA STĂNESCU
'Metamorphoses'

Changes

'Everything changes' – BRECHT

Nothing changes. You are just
The same. A glass of wine
Poured out with you tastes
As different, and words mean
My love neither more nor less.

A glass of wine tastes the same,
Just as neither more nor less
Words poured out with you
Mean you are different,
And my love changes nothing.

Thoughts

There are days when the mind grazes,
Circling itself like an answer
Lazily guessing its question.
How fragile they are, thoughts,
How delicately to be hoarded!
When a white thought runs away
It takes on the colour of air,
Of water. Unguarded thought,
Home thought in search of a heart,
Heartless thought in search of a home,
Desert thought thirsting for an oasis,
Pale fractured thought, let me catch you,
Name you and give you a colour.
Green thought, and you hide in leaves,
Black thought alone in darkness, butterfly thought
Deprived of your chrysalid memory –
Thought unexpressed like an unsown seed,
A shapeless chameleon thought
In a multitude of subtle poses.
Sublime, ridiculous thought
Unable to stand still! Bird thought adrift
In a continual migration towards a meaning,
And the meaning runs away and takes on the colour
Of thought. Intangible meaning, oasis
Thirsting for a desert, heart in search of a home,

Question circling an invisible answer
As ripples dwindle from a sinking stone –
Secret, unbridled meaning, quickly
Gather your thoughts, they are swarming. Lock
them away.

January

(TUNE: BACOVIAN)

The fugitive colours return:
A shadowy grey and yellow.
My spirits lurch alone
To the solemn fall of snow.

A song spins heavily round,
Rising thoughts beat slow
In tall columns of sound
To the solemn fall of snow.

And where was I in the night,
And where were you . . . Ah no,
All the words are taking flight
To the solemn fall of snow.

Stone-in-Oxney 1976

for Richard Holmes and Joanna Latimer

1 *At the Table*

In the bare, low-ceilinged attic
Of my friends' rented cottage, I sit
By the window at the old table with fake
Marble top and ill-fitting leaves, bought cheap
For the work I have too long put off.
Sharply the moon climbs out
Of the banked clouds wheeling across the hill;
In the crowded orchard, the pond
Shines with a ripple of shadows, yellow and black.
Here I have seen out the summer, watching
The far fields hazy-mauve in the afternoon,
The fireline creeping over the cropped hill –
Watching the last bright apple
Missed for a week by the pickers,
At the top of the nearest tree.

2 *At Such Times*

What more
Can you need at such times than
A room with an adequate table, bed
And chair comfortable enough,

A window for contemplating the slow
Turns of the day (far hills,
A great tree bending over a pond
And the voice of a shepherd calling his dog
As the sheep pass through the orchard
Suit me well, though you may imagine
Whatever you see fit), and friends
Downstairs or outside in the garden
Companionable with laughter,
The next meal in preparation,
And work to be done, not too much.

3 *Leaving*

When my work was done
And I moved out all my belongings
I left the table behind
In the attic. Let it stay
There, to be used or disposed of, sold
And bought cheaply again.
Say that it found its place.

Spring Scene, Wishful

Sun brings them out, the girls with bright faces
Unfurled as petals; they walk
Smiling with the spring in their step,
Wondering who might pick them.

Love Lent Me You for a Night

Dearest of friends, remember as your mind
Turns outward from an unexpected flight,
If it should close and lock you from the light
I offer you a key. Open your hand.

Music of the Spheres

When violin airs float over the hills
And long grass sighs and panpipes keen
A thin whistle of birdsong, your echoes
Come to me like the diminishing
Waves of a dead star
From a galaxy which has moved on.
I stand on a foreign hilltop
Catching the traces of wind.

Memories of the Earthquake

Bucharest. 4 March 1977

It was a perfect dazzling frosty night.
The moon large and crisp. Rats in the street
and in the gasworks; curious. A taxidriver
saw a cloud of gas the puzzled engineers
released; he wondered, then accelerated.
Supper-time. Cezar's dog began to howl. A minute more
and then the rumble, and then the shelves began
to juggle ornaments, the furniture
to shuffle round the room, stairways and floors
bulging like crazy mirrors...
The endless brief minute of life and death.
And whether you know that you are still alive,
whether the world is ending or goes on,
you freeze, then move in a mechanical panic.
Remember blankets, forget to lock the door.
Stumble out to the undulating streets
while buildings grind and shear and topple
in darkness as the electricity cuts.
In a tram stopped by the city cemetery,
a woman saw the gravestones dance to the moon
and cried, 'My God, now I believe in you...
forgive me for being a Party secretary...'
And then the muddled night of scouring rubble,
the heroism, the inefficiency,
the looting and the searching for lost friends:

rescuers crushed by falling masonry,
dogs sniffing out babies wrapped in blankets
from the cupboards their missing parents hid them in.
Count the dead, count the living, count the cost.
For those who perished, no memorials
save among all the awesome images,
the ruined streets, the unrepeatable noise
of death, the simple things that are recalled:

an ikon left unstolen on a wall.

Ring of Gold

Ring, ring of gold.
with a small stone at the heart,
I loved you, dearest thing,
but my luck was out.

White angels came to me
and settled on my heart,
I loved you, soul of mine,
but my luck was out.

Ripe quinces came to me
saying, Eat me, eat,
ring, ring of gold
with a small stone at the heart,

I loved you, dearest thing,
but my luck was out,
ring, ring of gold
with a small stone at the heart.

after a Romanian folk-song

Truth Games

1 *How to Tell Lies*

With a poker face
And a few well-timed grins –
Looking up with a sincere
Glance, just
As if you were telling the truth.

2 *Advice to Public Speakers*

Look serious. Cut out the jokes.
Bore us with official statistics
So that we have no doubt
Of your true command of the subject.
If possible, from time to time
Fart like a human being.

3 *An Exchange of Ideas*

We listen to the address.
Sensing our boredom, the speaker
Draws his sentences out
In polysyllabic, slow periphrases.
When at length he runs out of words

Our applause is very prolonged.
Thanking the speaker fulsomely, the chairman
Asks if we have any questions.
Silence. This is known
As an exchange of ideas.

4 *Question Time*

We won't ask awkward questions,
Naturally. They know
That we will be more embarrassed to ask
Serious, tough-sounding questions
Than they will be to trot out the trivial answers.
They answer our trivial questions
Very seriously.

5 *A Dialogue*

He lies with a faint smile,
We listen with controlled amazement.
To our dull, obvious questions
He gives the approved, dull answers:
We laugh, more at ourselves.
When he laughs, we will know
That he understands us exactly.

6 *The True Facts*

The way to tell lies in public
Is with a straight face.
The way to listen to lies in public
Is with a straight face.
If the true facts ever came out,
Everyone would crack with laughter.

Scene

A roof weighed down, then a door
Slammed with the burden of silence.
The sky's tense load, wave on wave.
Moonlight, the light of bereavement
Trickles in dusty gutters.
Half-darkness in bedrooms,
The strained tones of existence
Faintly, mutedly sounding.

after Faiz

The Words

The words have gone away,
They will not be back today.
They flew away like birds
Migrating in great clouds:
They have cold seas to cross,
Their fortune and their loss
Cannot be told, but tell
How when the sudden bell
Sounds a death or a birth
They echo on around the spinning earth.

Birdsong at Midnight

quod si prisca redit Venus . . .

Birdsong at midnight: on a balcony
    we sat above a field, fresh haystacks pale
in the play of moonlight, fluctuating shadow
    of clouds and trees that fringed the field; only
a low babble of frogs from the stream beyond
    disturbed the yellow stillness. Then the sudden
riff of a nightingale split the silence,
    cutting us to the quick.
                                        As if time
stopped and gave itself to us, we flew
    in ceaseless chirruping conversations,
merged and were submerged in birdsong. Love
    settled on us for a spell, we basked
in it like the blest, shone like the full
    moon in the honeysuckle fragrance.

Another place, a colder midnight now;
    it is New Year's Day, nineteen eighty-four,
a time to reckon with, a birdless time.
    Stupidity! It was no nightingale;
I have not heard the song-thrush now for months,
    and keep the wild voices of birds at bay
for fear love will encircle me again
    alone. I think of you, reach out – draw back,

thinking of a death two weeks ago
        though the news reached me only yesterday.
'Enkidu is dead, my friend who used
        to kill lions with me.' In my head I still
talk with him as I've done these last years,
        all that has changed is a postcard came.
What if it hadn't? Would he be alive
        like those you love but cannot often see,
a cherished state of heart that's realized
        in prospect or in memory, – like a chord
once struck which, though its echo fades in space,
        sounds in the mind again with perfect pitch
the notes that ring unfathomably true.
        Death is an absence. Absences in life
mean we live nearer death than we acknowledge.
        I cannot prove you are still alive,
take it for granted as I took my friend's
        presence as read – until the postcard came.
How should I mourn beyond the reach of words?
        How should we honour death, its debt to life?
I trust the music of the nightingale
        by any name, the unpredictable
promise that quickens when two people meet
        and know the moment, though it vanishes,
hints at the recreation of their lives.
        Observe the silence that surrounds the music.
Name the unnameable. Enkidu my friend
        is dead, let the lions lie with lambs.

Our time will come.
'Or simply the fact that you
exist stirs the world here and now.'
You haunt me like the memory of that friend
whose voice I heard in the monastery silence,
in the quick tongues of birds in the rose-garden,
as we dissolved our spirits in each other.
Love settled on us for a little while,
we shook it off. 'Blessèd are they that mourn.'
The pure unearthly keening of panpipes
brings me closer to things far from you...

And you don't know that I am sitting here
writing to you; that all my thoughts are poised
to speak, as I often cannot face to face,
clearly and say the things I want to say.
How intimately you are with me now!
I think of you, catch you this way and that,
try you in different attitudes: silent, talking,
sober, laughing, serious or drunk,
still or in motion: a kaleidoscope
of versions of you plays across my mind.
And then I stop it: how, love, do you live
in me? In letters, memory, or
when I telephone you and your voice summons
your being to me instantaneously:
then the good minute goes. We only live
together when we know we live at one,

when the moment no longer disappears
    but strikes the same note. I would do so now,
settling in silence for what's understood,
    what you alone can read between the lines.

To a Murderer

for Colin Caffell, in memory of Sheila, Daniel and Nicholas Caffell, June and Neville Bamber, shot 6–7 August 1985

A sunflower strains to heaven, then hangs its head.
In summer's last, belated blaze of light
The morning glories trumpet till they fade...
You have denied them this: denied them day and night.

Schoolchildren fool and chatter in the park,
Grownups remind themselves that life goes on
In spite of everything: but in what dark
And unimaginable undertaking have they gone?

A fox howls near my door, then slinks off, stunned.
Worms rot the grounded apples to their core.
Anger burns coldly and consumes the mind;
Existence shrinks to hollow places, nothing more.

Sooner or later we must all be dead.
But morning glories rise along the wall
When their time comes, and sunflowers have their head...
Know that the dead are praying, murderer, on your soul.

Discovery

Years of stubborn defence
in a cramped position.
                                        Then, slow
expansion in the centre,
watchfully guarding the flanks.
Patience in time-trouble: hold
fast.
          But all at once
something, I don't know what, moved
out of the way, the lines
cracked and are gaping open.
Capture me gently, queen.

Sprachlos

in memoriam Rolf Bossert, 1952–1986

Rolf, *we have not met*
though we embraced on parting
you were not there and
though we shared bread and wine
I was not there
though we shared a table with friends and
you would say nothing
though we shook hands on meeting

A stone, unblinking

(you would not tell me what they did to you
no one could tell just what they did to you
they will tell no one what they did to you)

sunk without tremor or trace

Tell me no more now, Rolf,
you have said too much.
By your ice-blue eyes and blazing beard
Rolf, tell us of nothing.

Forgiveness

for J. B.

Since your life is already a living hell
I cannot wish you damnation.

Ghost

God's concentration slips –

God is everywhere, God is absent,
God is on the gallows

refusing to die, God wants
his birthright, to live for ever –

but most of all God just
wants to be dead, not to suffer

like a child, but to suffer his children
coming to him – to be host

to the numbered and the unnumbered,
not to be tied down like this,

to be deaf to everything –
and finally, numb with the pain

of the painless, God finds the ghost
to give up, a tiny ghost, dumb

with radiant terror – God
turns a blind eye, gives it up

and gives us the slip again.

Weeping

A. O.

I wept. First
for myself, for all
my failings, my
failures, for
my life.

Then I wept for yours.

A Blessing

J. P.

In a year of mixed fortunes
you are my neat whisky,
an unmixed blessing.

The Finest Thing

Some say parades of cavalry, some foot soldiers,
others a fleet of ships…
tanks arrayed in Red Square,
flypasts by the Red Arrows, the Henley regatta…

But the finest thing on earth
is still whatever you love, and I would give
all the wealth of America
to see Julia's hair in sunlight or
hear Alison's laughter.

Small Hours

And is she sleeping tight
while the moon looms large,
in whose arms will she wake
and stretch to greet the bright
welcome of daybreak?

Keys

A closed book a window shut
a locked room

a window's unclear mirror
a dark room an unturned page

an unsealed window a page re-read
a room revealed

A door has opened

Bliss

I perch on the brink
of entering your life,
my open book.

The buzz of human sounds,
the buzz of machines,
swishing of trees.

I perch on the brink
of entering
your open book, my life.

The lake. Sun and moon.
Entrances to things, the moment
of entrance. Entrancement.

I perch on the brink
of entering your life,
your open book.

The Badness

Tell me for goodness' sake, where does it start?
And where on earth can it end?
The badness comes and goes. It hangs around...
But when it seems to have gone, it reappears,
the badness that is in the human heart,
the badness without end –

tell me, what is its power, its self-styled glory,
this badness which is half the human story?
It must start somewhere, it must have a source.
The badness grows and grows and grows its force.

Love is bitter…

Love is bitter, love is blind,
words mean nothing any more,
music, heartless and unkind,
sweetens sadness to the core.

Magical and meaningless
love springs like self-seeded plants,
growing where not quite expected,
smothering what it supplants.

Love doesn't last, it goes its own way.
Some say it's cruel to be kind.
Love goes on changing day by day.
Never mind.

Freeze

A glass of wine, a gas fire,
there's nothing more to hope for.

Bitter days, the mind
winds up and will not unwind,

verses stiffen and make no sense,
all the poets lose all credence.

Music will not warm the air.
You sit and stare and stare and stare,

longing for consuming heat
as ice bites slowly at the heart.

Accounting

Assets, one stubborn heart –
stock falling, estimated
at the lower of tears
and unrealizable worth.
Income: uncertain, intangible,
high interest, low returns.
Expenses, a waste of shame.

Sundry accruals discounted,
some debts not quite written off.
The cost of souls, hope and fear.
Numerous problematic
transactions put in suspense.
Profit and loss, to be determined
by independent audit.

Something is wrong on the balance sheet,
there is an item missing.

Flying

My dreams of flying were never
As beautiful as the flight
Of the balsa-wood model gliders my father
Patiently built me, covered
With translucent papery skin –
Propellers powered by rubber bands,
They flew in glorious loops
Over and over
Until they plummeted beyond repair.

At school I learned about falling
And the fall, which I disbelieved.
But the principles of flight
Defeated me. Much later
I learnt that falling in love
Is flight, or a flight, or a fall, with luck
Beyond, over and over, looping and out.

Oooh Aaah

for Euro 96

Where are the golden boys time cannot scar,
has the grim striker swept them all from view?
But where, O where is Eric Cantona?

The ghost of White Hart Lane, John White, a star
in any firmament, red white or blue –
where are the golden boys time cannot scar?

On what Elysian pitch or in what bar
do they find space to push their passes through?
But where, O where is Eric Cantona?

The sweeper took our skipper: Bobby, are
you sweetly tackling heavenly forwards too?
Where are the golden boys time cannot scar?

The hand of God has scored but cannot mar
those Babes of '58 whose bliss we knew.
But where, O where is Eric Cantona?

Angelic wing-halves watching from afar,
the final whistle blew for all of you.
Where are the golden boys time cannot scar?
But where, O where is Eric Cantona?

A Little Summer Madness

My dear, I simply don't know what to do.
It's most unlike me, honestly, and so
I think I may be falling in love with you.

What to think? What to say? I haven't a clue,
I'm jelly-limbed, soft in the head, and O
Good Lord, I simply don't know what to do.

My brain spins round and round! Such a to-do,
It's crazy but I'm laughing. Here we go,
Looks like I could be falling in love with you.

Okay, it's silly, I can't think it through.
I wish that this had happened years ago...
Damn it, I simply don't know what to do.

And yes, life's complicated, that is true –
It's bits of happiness and bits of woe.
Bugger – I might be falling in love with you.

I'm in a tiz, I'm drinking Special Brew,
Everything has your name on it, your glow.
Oh shit, I simply don't know what to do.
I think I must be falling in love with you.

Some Blue Perhaps

I have forgotten how to write love poems.
When I was young I would lose my way
night after night in their maze

of rhymes, searching for the vain
chimera of alchemy that would turn
poetry into love day after day

or love into a poem. I daydream now
of what I might put in a poem
for you. A curtain, some blue perhaps,

a good night's sleep, the smile
in a photograph, a few
potatoes, something I cannot think of

and a stone, the heart of a stone.

Spell to Make Time Pass

Hurry seconds, minutes fly,
Clock, tick faster, help time by,
Spin more quickly, hours, go –
Time is relative, but slow.
Morning slip to afternoon,
Evening fall to darkness soon,
Day again – and one day less
Brings me nearer happiness.
Make this day a yesterday,
Let tomorrow be today,
Change the daytime into night,
Bring me home my love tonight.

Scraps

I stumbled in the middle of my life

Poetry does not come as naturally
as leaves to a tree, as weeds to a flower-bed,
as greenfly to the roses.

I cannot speak the words for things I feel,
how can I know that what I feel is real?

You go so far and then you turn away.
It makes no sense
                                        coming all this way
And going back.

You go so far and then you turn away.
However near you are you will not stay.

Angels

Such a flutter of wings

A preparatory flutter of wings
A perfunctory flutter of wings

Soul of a Smile

Upturned buttercup,
I beam into your eyes –
two butterflies shine!

I never knew the colour of her eyes
Eyes gazing inward, shutters of the soul

This summer which is over will not leave me.
Day by day its shadows lengthen and
still longer shadows are thrown on the ground.

So far from you, I don't know where I am.
Where you are – where were you? I've lost track.
The words are short, the words keep coming back.
I do not understand them, I am dumb.
How far my life has gone away from home.

What if the old love does not return . . .
We live in angled mirrors reflecting
corridors of the past.

You well up in my soul
a hidden spring
gushing out of control

I am in love, in love, in love, in love.
We have a chance, we will be hand in glove.

This is the word made ink,
it will float on the page or sink

Sorrow lies on my heart
        like a secret burden
Sorrow lies on my mind
        like a detached memory
Sorrow lies on my body
        like an empty weight

Peace to our warring hearts, our souls
that ache for the vision of that lost
elysium of total trust,
when time was endless and we knew
nothing and everything was true

You know the words don't mean a thing they say
or say a thing they mean
and things don't mean a word they say.

The words don't mean a thing they say,
and things don't say a word they mean.
Nothing I say means anything to you, or me.

Cover me over, night,
let me sink,
mother, a stone wrapped
into the white
trap that sucks the breath
from the quick and lights
the dead into the dark.

Wide-eyed beguiling
love steals my soul,
a woman

comes to me, her
eyes fraught with pain,
her longing

straight as a child's.
Who can retain
his resolution?

Guile-weaver, trap-spinner, snare-maker, spell-binder:
Aphrodite by Sappho, or something like.

Brittle Madonna,
angel of metal,
frangible heart,
heart of love and hate
intangible.

In the yellow silence I examine
the currency of her soul,
balancing colours and shapes.
I ripple the pool of silence.
Having no words
I give you my silence, thoughts
that slip through the mind
like sand through the fingers.

Word after word. Words.
And silence, before, after.
And beyond words, beyond
silence, as it was
in the beginning, as
it shall be ever after.

A heart in winter
cracks like a windowpane,
it shrinks, it shrivels
to its core of stone.

In chilling weather
watch the soul wither.

No, it is not like that;
a heart of glass
brittle and tense
splits like a chunk of ice.

My wife sleeps sound upstairs,
my daughter in her cot.
I live here happily
and I wish it were not so.

My love, the love I cannot love
is years away and oh
I wish it were not so,
I wish it were not so.

The treeboat is at anchor.
Harboured in your arms
I cast off in my dreams.

Steer me through deep branches:
let me swim and sink in you
till the treeboat comes to rest.

In the treeboat let me sink
to the riverbed of your heart.

Notes

These are not the poems I had hoped to write, but those that I managed to.

To separate the poems of my first collection, now minus its concluding frivolities, from the later poems, I have added an intermediate group of translations, some of which point to poems elsewhere in the collection.

Many poems, not only my own, have shadowy influences or antecedents. Translating or making versions or adaptations of poems has been for me a form of keeping in touch with poetry when I could not otherwise write verse. Like writing 'original' poetry, it has been an end and a pleasure in itself, both as an exploration and a reclaiming.

Shifting Frontiers

21 'Remembering' departs from a well-known poem by Pushkin. Anachronisms, an altered ending and a different metre disqualify it as translation.

22 'Envy' is also too changed metrically to be regarded as translation, although it gives the matter of Yevtushenko's poem (*Zavist'*) straightforwardly.

29 'Fear' was the subject set for the Newdigate Prize for Poetry in 1965. The regulations stated that entries are 'not to exceed 300 lines; the metre is not restricted to heroic couplets, but dramatic form of composition is not allowed.'

39 'Homage to Mimnermos' is a patchwork from some of the surviving fragments of the greatest early elegiac poet, Mimnermos of Colophon, who flourished in the late seventh century BC.

45 'Ezra Pound 1970' was written for a special Pound issue of *Agenda* in response to William Cookson's request for a review of *Drafts & Fragments of Cantos CX–CXVII*. It also uses the *cento* (patchwork) technique.

51 'Six Poems after Faiz' took texts from a bilingual edition of the Urdu poet (1911–1984) as their point of departure. One or two of the pieces are versions of whole poems; others are freely adapted or combined from different poems.

55 'In Memory of Pastoral' borrows lines (1, 3–4) remembered from Cyril Connolly. Theokritos lived and wrote for some years on the island of Kos; the poet Meleager spent much of his life there. 'Long live 21 April 1967' (the date of the Colonels' takeover) is by now, I imagine, long effaced from the hillside.

Intermezzo

Most of these versions are indebted to the work of other writers and scholars, and to those who helped me with the languages that I don't know: among them Margitt Lehbert (Brecht), Virgil Nemoianu (Bacovia), Petru Popescu (Stănescu), Peter Sherwood (Pilinszky) and the late János Csokits and Támas Marx (Pilinszky, *Crater*).

78 My version of *The Song of Songs* (1975) owed much to Robert Gordis's *The Song of Songs: A New Study, Translation and Commentary*, New York, 1954.

78 Sappho, for many the greatest of Greek lyric poets, was born on Lesbos and lived *c.* 630–570 BC.

79 Horace, friend of Vergil and one of Rome's greatest poets, lived 65–8 BC. The poems are *Odes* 3.13 and 4.7.

81 Hadrian, born in 76 AD, was Roman Emperor from 117 until his death in 138. He is supposed to have written this poem shortly before dying.

82 Sulpicius Lupercus Servasius Iunior, if that is his true name, lived in the 4th century AD. Two poems by him survive.

83 Li Yu lived *c.* 937–978. He was the third and last ruler of the Southern Tang dynasty from 961–976.

84 François Villon, born in Paris in 1431, wrote *Le Grand Testament*, from which this ballade is taken, in 1461.

86 Alexander Puskhin, Russia's greatest poet, lived from 1799 to 1837.

87 Gérard de Nerval (1808–1855) is best known for his autobiographical *Aurélia*, the novella *Sylvie* and the sonnet sequence *Les Chimères*.

88 The Romanian poet George Bacovia lived 1881–1957. The poems are from his first book *Plumb* (Lead), 1916.

89 Nichita Stănescu, Romania's most extraordinary post-war poet, lived 1933–1983.

90 The Hungarian poet János Pilinszky lived 1921–1981. 'Master Me' is the opening poem in his first collection *Trapéz és korlát* (Trapeze and Parallel Bars), 1946. 'Pathogeny and Swansong' is from his last, *Kráter* (Crater), 1975.

92 Bertolt Brecht (1898–1956) was often considered to be a greater poet than playwright. *Poems 1913–1956* (1976) edited by John Willett and Ralph Manheim is a compendium of his poems in English translation.

Changes

104 'Memories of the Earthquake' evokes through others' memories the aftermath of the Romanian earthquake of 4 March 1977. Among more than 1,500 dead were the poet Veronica Porumbacu and her husband, the literary critic Mihai Petroveanu, who were hosting a dinner party, and all their guests who included the poet A.E. Baconsky.

106 'Ring of Gold': I have never been able to find a Romanian original for this song, 'Inel de aur', reconstructed from my memory of hearing Nichita Stănescu sing it. It may have been his own composition.

112 'Birdsong at Midnight': the epigraph means 'what if the old love returns' (Horace *Odes* 3.9).

116 'To a Murderer' is in memory of my niece and her two children who died, along with her adoptive parents, at the hand of Jeremy Bamber in the White House Farm murders, 7 August 1985.

117 'Discovery' is a term in chess for an attack unmasked by the move of an intervening piece.

118 'Sprachlos' remembers the German-language Romanian poet Rolf Bossert who committed suicide in Frankfurt shortly after leaving Ceauşescu's Romania.

122 'The Finest Thing' and 'Small Hours' allude to well-known fragments of Sappho.

130 'Oooh Aaah' remembers some great footballers of the past, among them the late England captain Bobby Moore and John White of Scotland and Spurs, who died aged 27 from a lightning strike. His stealthy running gave him the nickname 'the ghost'. I saw him score the final goal in Tottenham's 8–1 win over Gornik Zabrze at White Hart Lane in September 1961.

The title is from the chant 'Oooh aaah, Cantona', with the accent on the final syllable. The Manchester United star turned actor and singer, who famously said 'When seagulls follow the trawler, it's because they think sardines will be thrown into the sea', was controversially left out of the French squad for Euro 96.

ACKNOWLEDGEMENTS

Poems in *Shifting Frontiers* appeared, sometimes in earlier versions, in these publications: *Agenda*, *Carcanet*, *Isis*, *La Liberté* (Canada), The Poetry Book Society's *New Poems 1973*, The Arts Council of Great Britain's *New Poetry 1*, *The Oxford Magazine*, *PN Review*, *The Poetry Review*, *Priapus*, *Solstice* and the *Times Literary Supplement*. One or two were broadcast on the BBC's *Poetry Now*. Nineteen were published by Malcolm Rutherford as *Lifelines* (Satis, 1977), edited by Matthew Mead. A number of the poems were written or rewritten in 1975 under the genial auspices of the International Writing Program at the University of Iowa, directed by the late Paul and Hualing Nieh Engle.

Versions in the 'Intermezzo' section appeared in *Agenda*, *Arion*, *Iowa Review*, *Isis* and the *Times Literary Supplement*. Poems in the final section appeared in *The Independent*'s 'Poem of the Day', *Iowa Review*, *The Literary Review*, *PN Review* and in Colin Caffell's *In Search of the Rainbow's End* (1994).

My thanks to all the editors, and for critical and other help over the years to many friends, especially Gavin Bantock, John Birtwhistle, Richard Holmes, Anthony Howell, Michael Schmidt and those no longer with us, Harry Guest, Lee Harwood, Peter Levi and Jacky Simms. And especially to Julia Sterland who helped to put this book together.

INDEX OF TITLES

About the Author

PETER JAY was born in 1945 in Chester. He was educated at Lancing College and Lincoln College, Oxford where he studied Classics and English. Shortly after graduating he founded Anvil Press Poetry as a specialist poetry publisher. It ran from 1968 to 2016, when it ceased operation and was subsumed by Carcanet Press. He lives in Greenwich, south-east London.

He received the Newdigate Prize for Poetry in 1965 and a Rockefeller Foundation grant in 1968. He was Assistant Director for the London Poetry International Festivals from 1969–73. He was a member of the International Writing Program at the University of Iowa in 1975 and Visiting Lecturer in the Department of English at Iowa in 1980 and 1982, when he ran the Translation Workshop.

By Peter Jay

VERSE

Lifelines, Satis, 1977
Shifting Frontiers, Carcanet Press, 1980

TRANSLATIONS

Adonis & Venus, Work in Progress, Santa Barbara, 1968
The Song of Songs, Anvil, 1975
Nichita Stănescu: *The Still Unborn About the Dead* (with Petru Popescu), Anvil, 1975
Ştefan Aug. Doinaş: *Alibi and other poems* (with Virgil Nemoianu), Anvil, 1975
János Pilinszky: *Crater*, Anvil, 1978
George Bacovia: *Violet Dusk* (with Virgil Nemoianu), Editura Minerva, Bucharest, 1981
János Pilinszky: *Conversations with Sheryl Sutton* (with Éva Major), Carcanet Press, 1992
A Greek Garland, Greville Press, 2009

AS EDITOR

The Greek Anthology, Allen Lane and Penguin Books, 1973, 1981
The Poems of Meleager (with Peter Whigham), Anvil, 1975
Peter Russell: *All for the Wolves*, Anvil, 1984
Sappho Through English Poetry (with Caroline Lewis), Anvil, 1996
The Spaces of Hope, Anvil, 1998
Walt Whitman: *I Hear America Singing*, Anvil, 2001
Sally Purcell: *Collected Poems*, Anvil, 2002
The Sea! The Sea!, Anvil, 2005

Grey Suit Editions

GREY SUIT EDITIONS began as a video magazine in the 1990s. This featured avant-garde performance art, poetry and experimental film and music. These videos can be found on our website. Today we host an archive of the video footage as well as publishing books of literary interest and poetry chapbooks.

DONALD GARDNER *New and Selected Poems*
ANTHONY HOWELL *Collected Longer Poems*
ANTHONY HOWELL *The Distance Measured in Days* (NOVEL)
ANTHONY HOWELL *The Step is the Foot* (DANCE AND ITS RELATIONSHIP TO POETRY)
GWENDOLYN LEICK *Franckstrasse 31*
GWENDOLYN LEICK *Gertrude Mabel May* (AN ABC OF GERTRUDE STEIN'S LOVE TRIANGLE)
WALTER OWEN *The Cross of Carl: An Allegory* (PREFACE BY GEN. SIR IAN HAMILTON)
DAVID PLANTE *Essential Stories*
ILIASSA SEQUIN *Collected Complete Poems*

We also publish chap-books by Donald Gardner, Alan Jenkins, Fawzi Karim, Lorraine Mariner, Kerry-Lee Powell, Pamela Stewart, Rosanne Wasserman and Hugo Williams.

For further information visit
https://greysuiteditions.co.uk